SPORTS MEDICINE

for kids

First paperback edition October 2024

Book design by Betty Nguyen & Brandon Pham

ISBN 978-1-957557-31-1 (paperback)

Printed in the United States of America

Published by Black Phoenix Press

www.mdforkids.org

To the friends and family who have supported and loved us unconditionally, and to the mentors who have guided and taught us more than we could have imagined:

Thank you.

Betty & Brandon

Sports Medicine

(sports MEH-duh-sn)

the branch of medicine concerned with the diagnosis, treatment, and prevention of injuries related to sports and physical activity

Sports are physical activities or games that we play to have fun, get exercise, and compete with others.

Athletes are people who play sports. There are many types of sports, including football, basketball, baseball, and soccer!

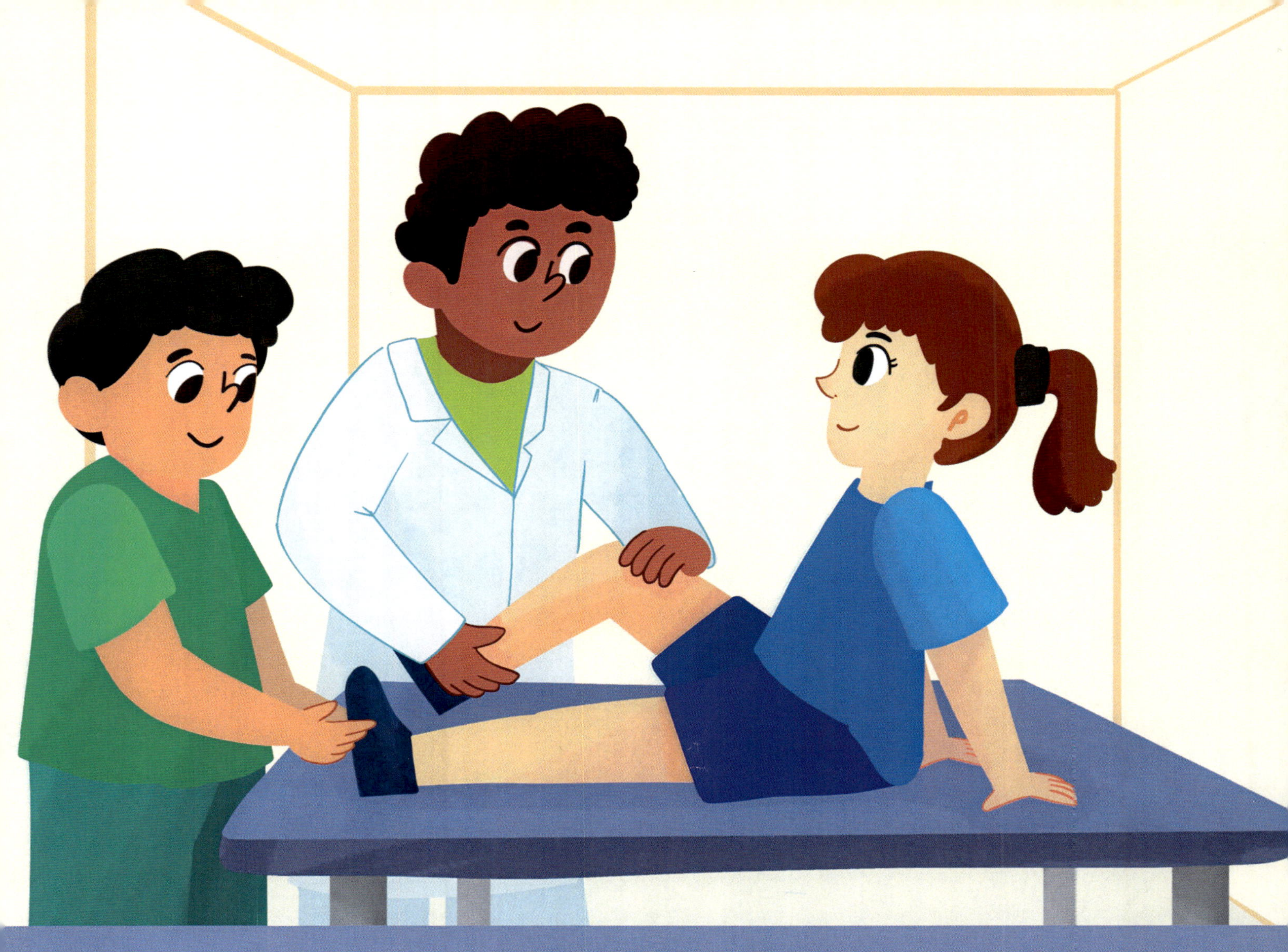

Sports medicine doctors prevent, diagnose, and treat injuries related to sports and physical activity.

Bones are the hard white tissues
that hold our body together.

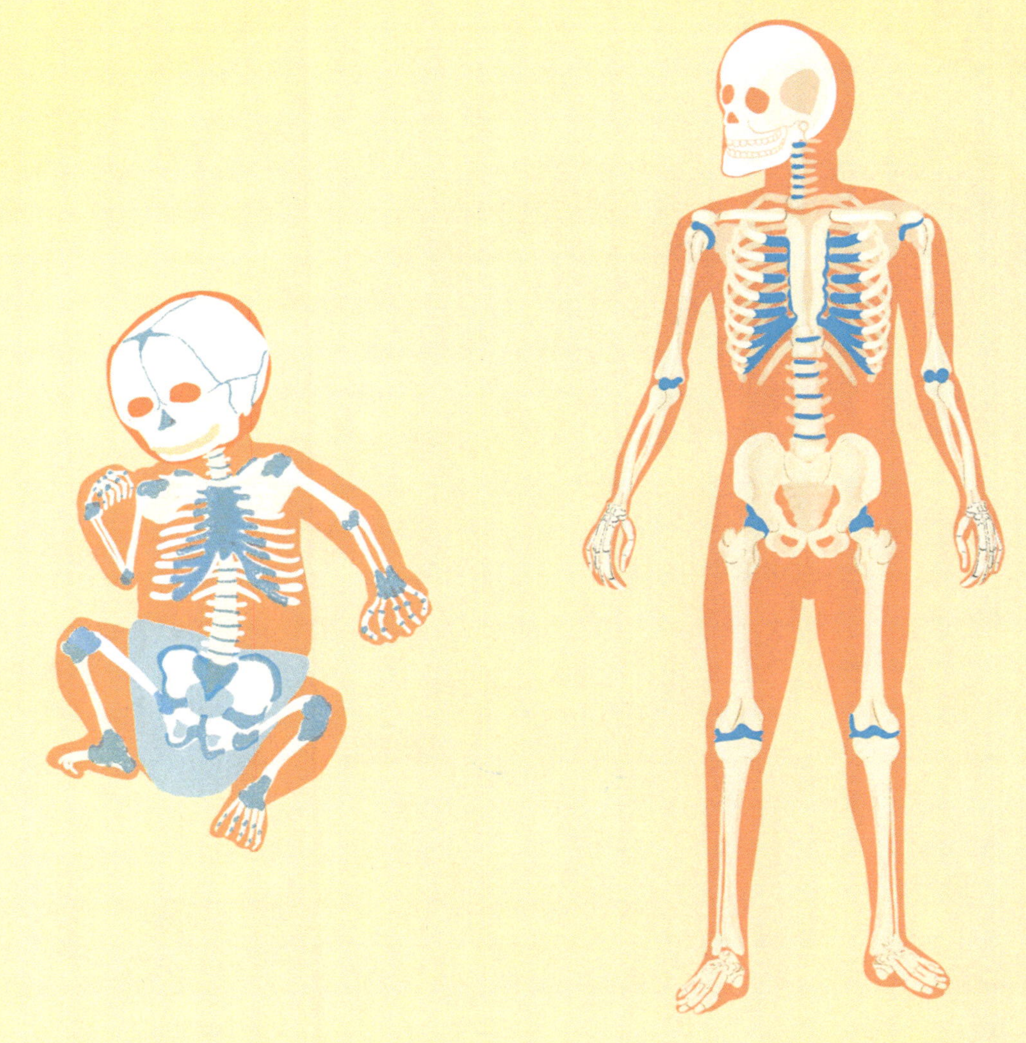

Together, our bones make up our **skeleton**.
As we get older, our bones fuse together.
That's why kids have more bones than adults!

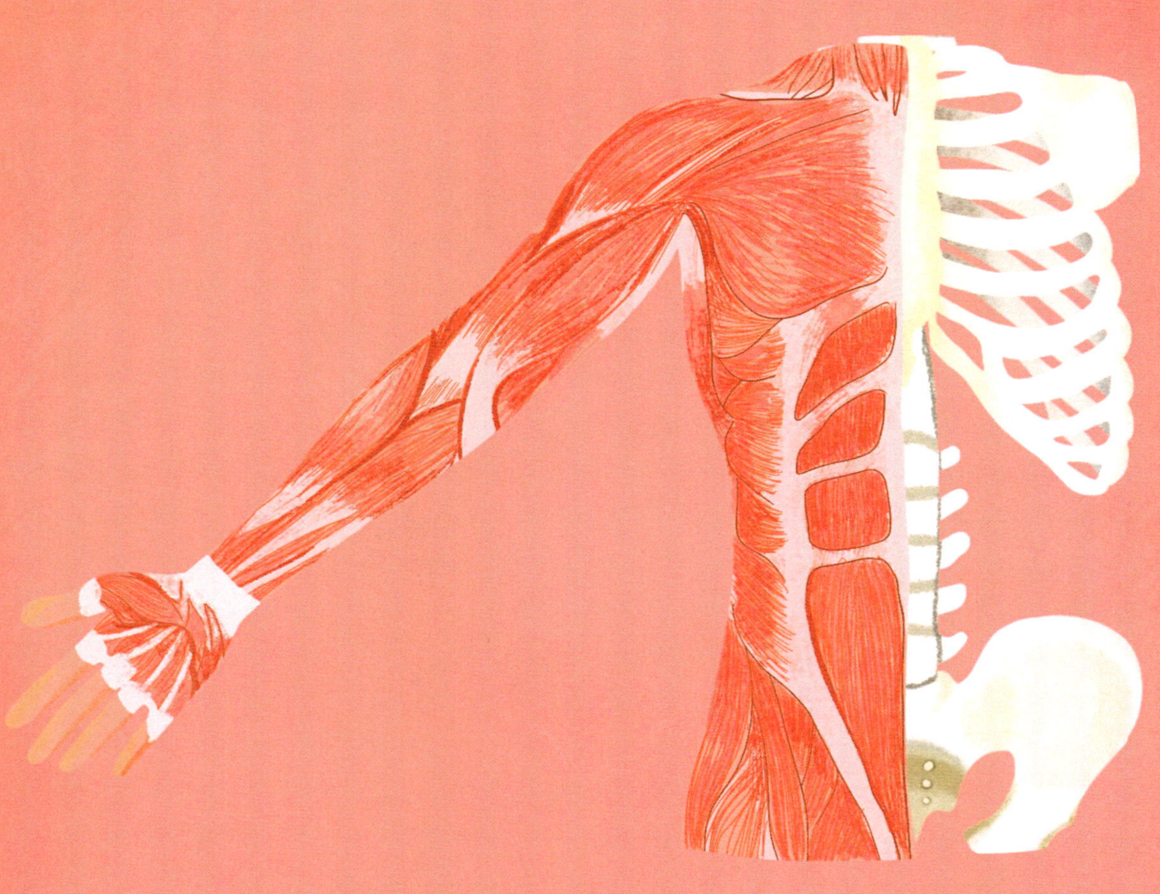

Muscles are the fibers that contract and produce motion in our body. There are three types of muscle.

Types of muscle

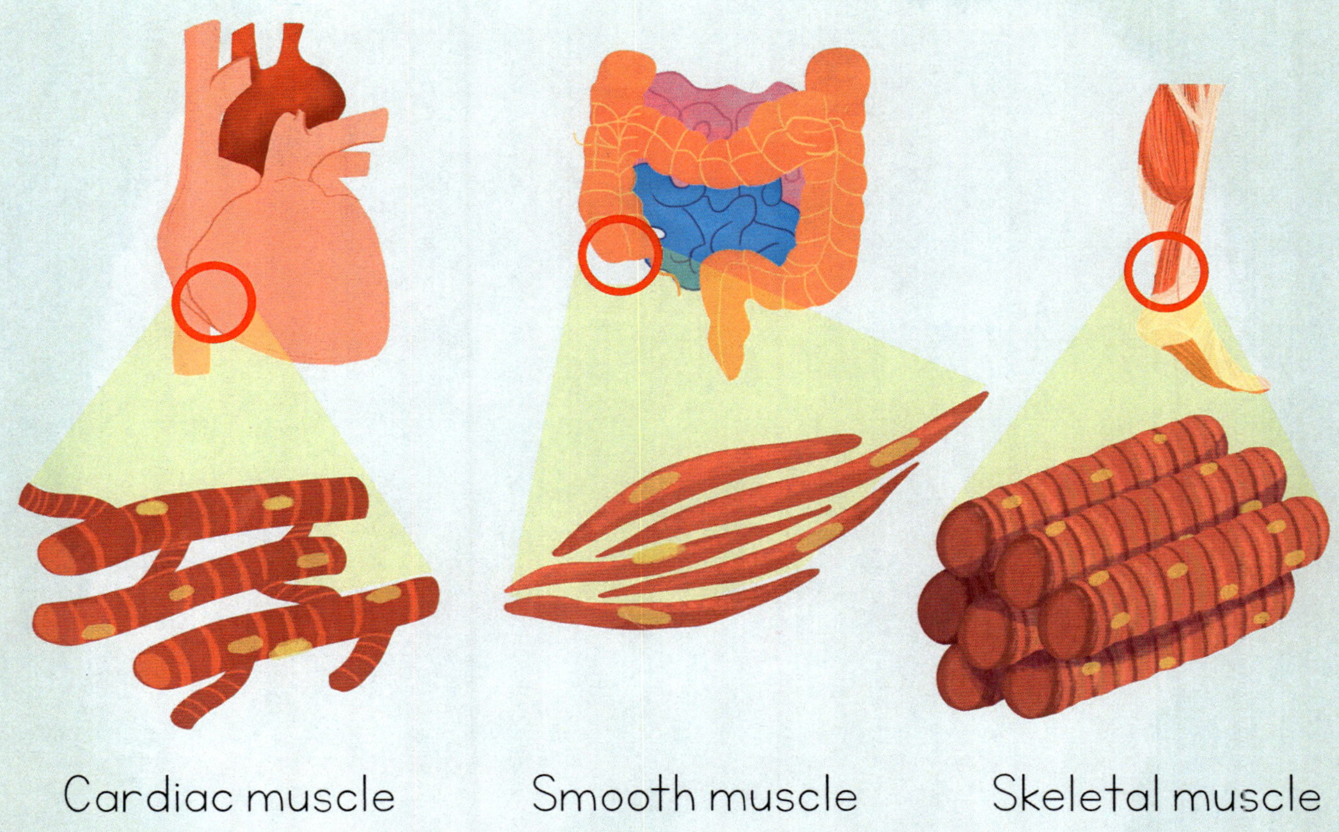

Cardiac muscle | Smooth muscle | Skeletal muscle

Cardiac muscle pumps blood to our body.

Smooth muscle moves food through our gut.

Skeletal muscle allows our body to move.

Joints

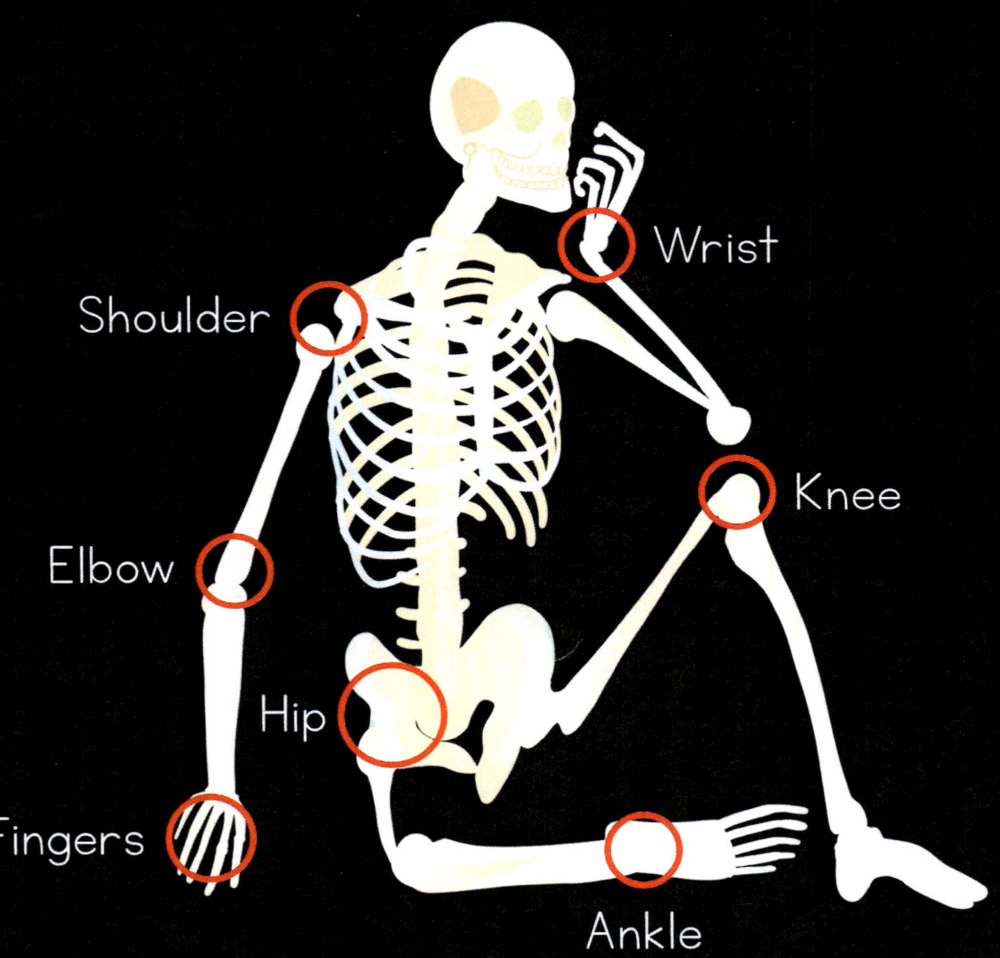

A **joint** is where two or more bones meet.
Joints help us bend our arms and legs.

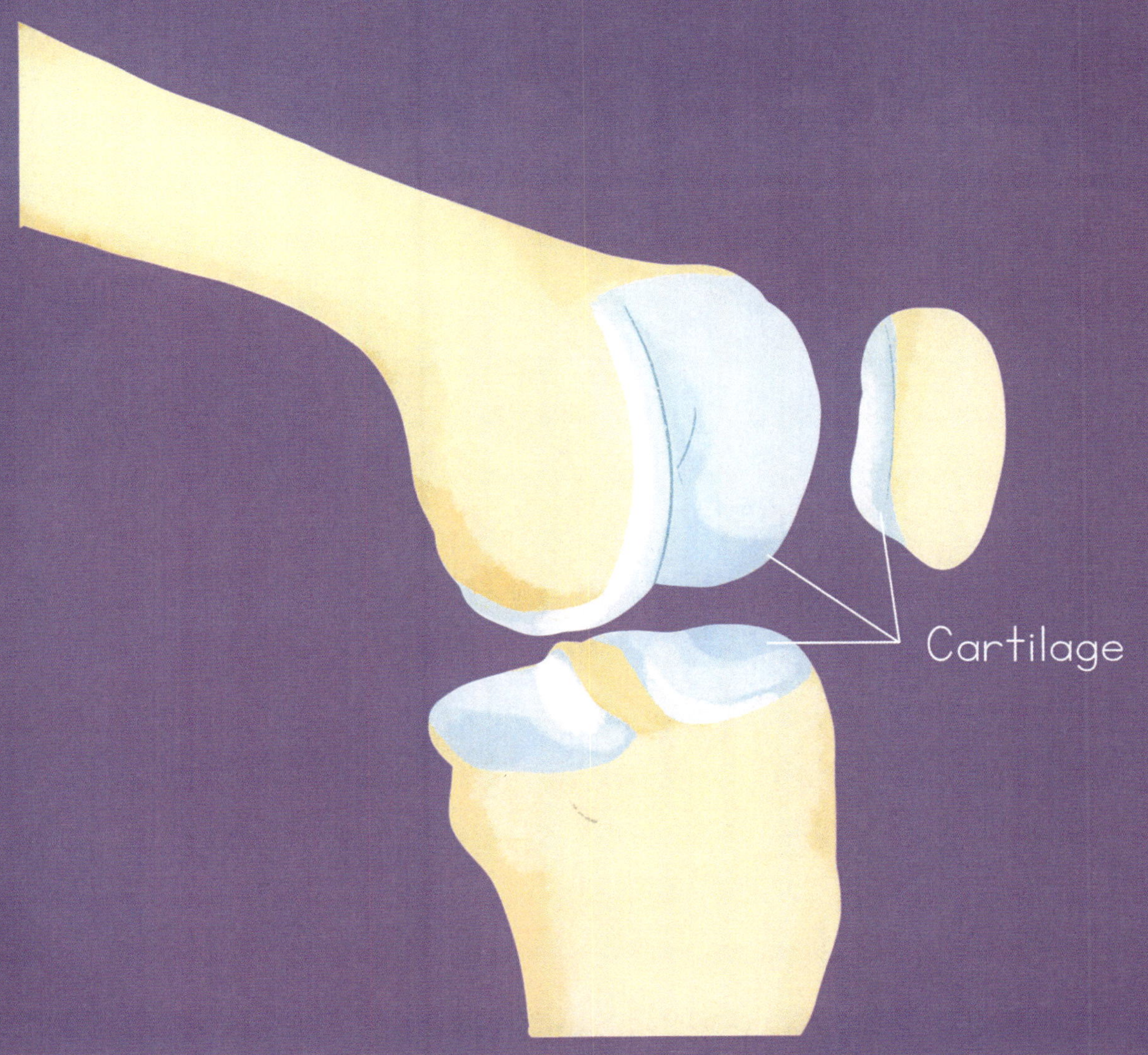

The ends of our bones at most joints are covered in a material called **cartilage**, which is like a cushion that protects our joints.

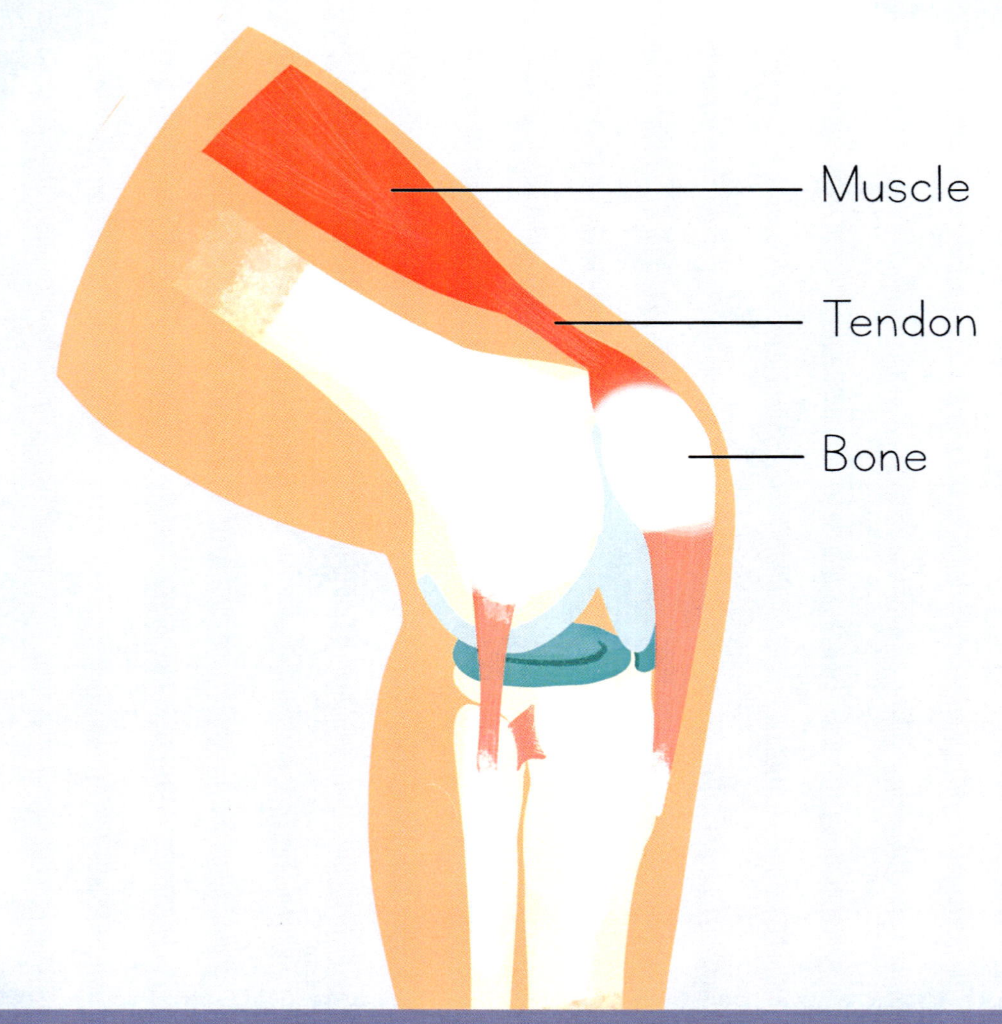

Tendons are tissues that connect muscle to bone. They allow movement to occur at our joints.

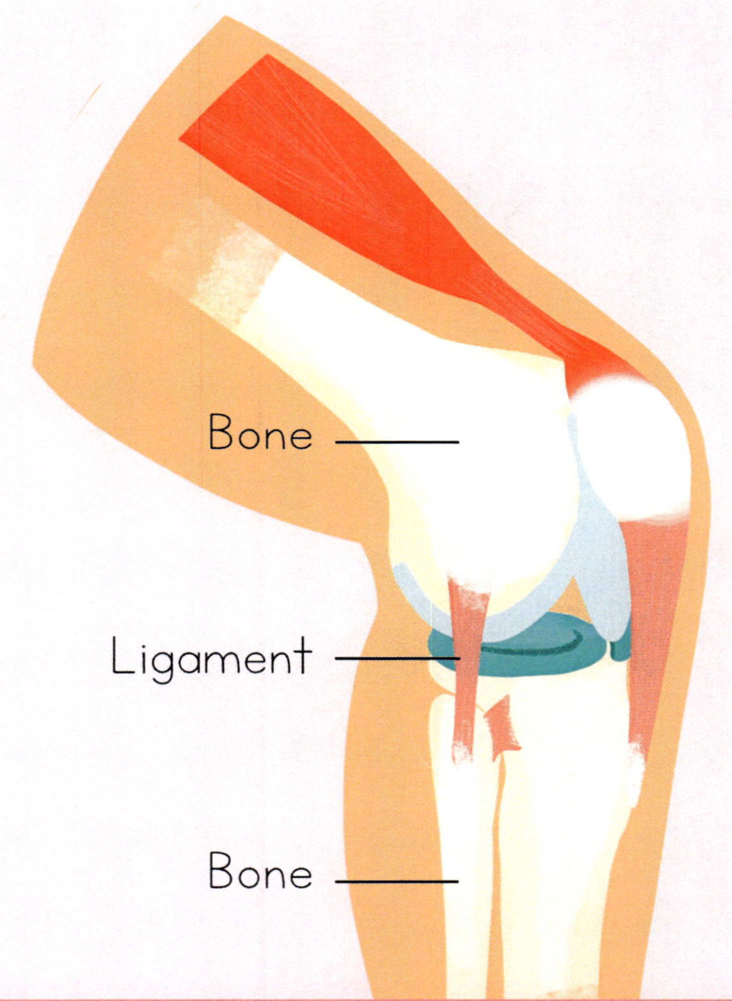

Ligaments are tissues that connect one bone to another bone. They help keep our joints stable.

Strain

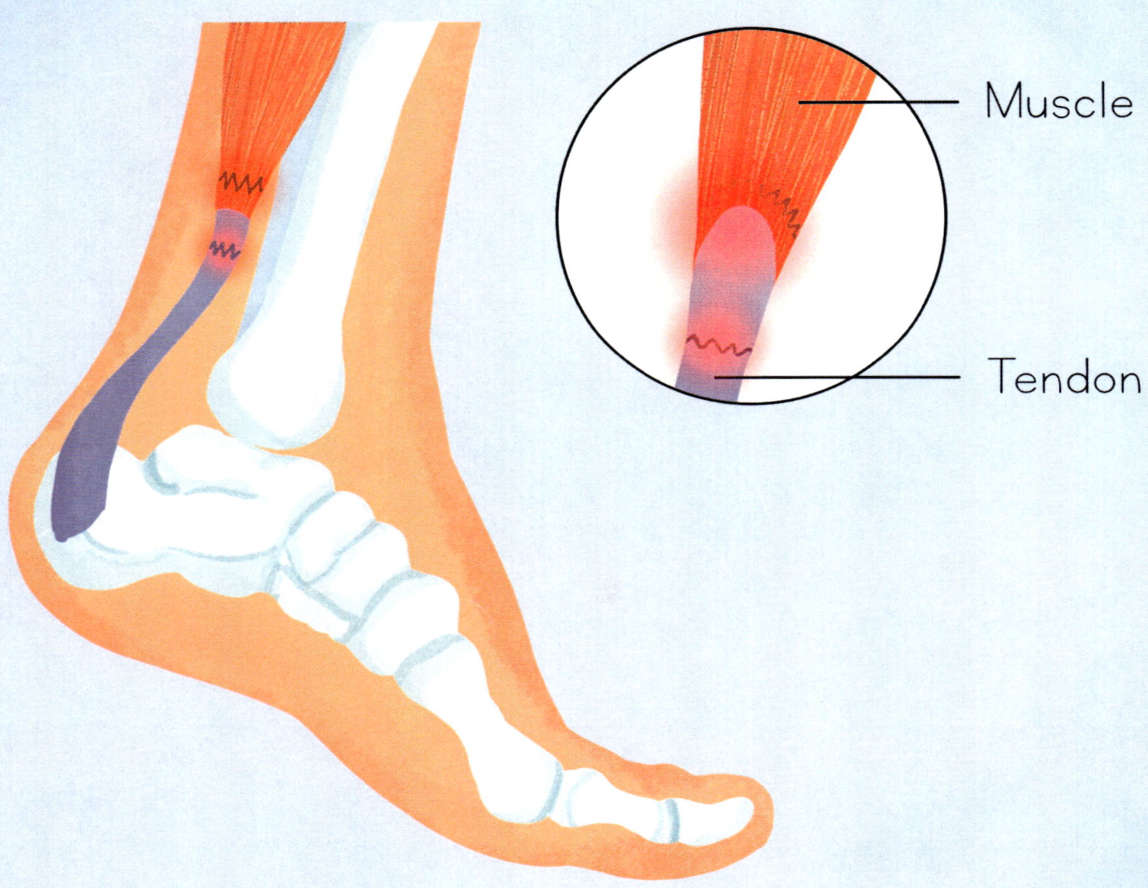

A **strain** is an injury that occurs when a *muscle* or *tendon* is stretched or torn.

Sprain

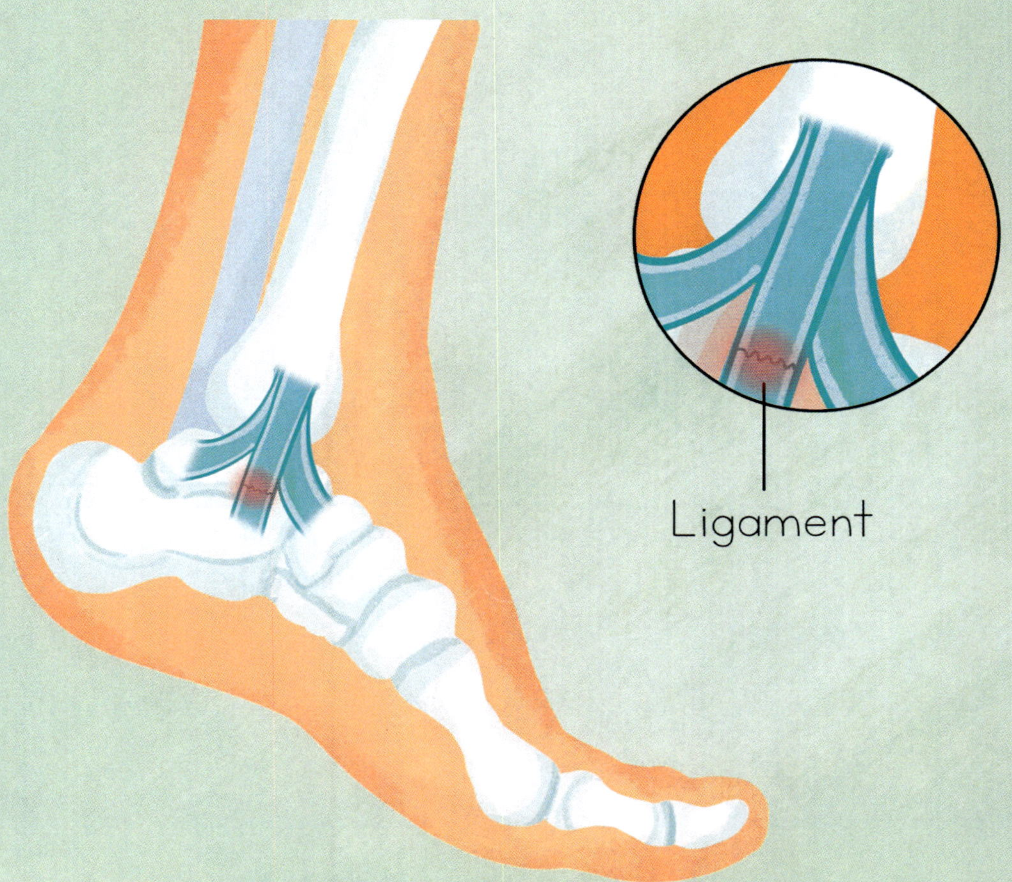

A **sprain** is an injury that occurs when a *ligament* is stretched or torn.

The most common sprain is an **ankle sprain**. This is from twisting the foot inward or outward more than it normally can.

Tendonitis

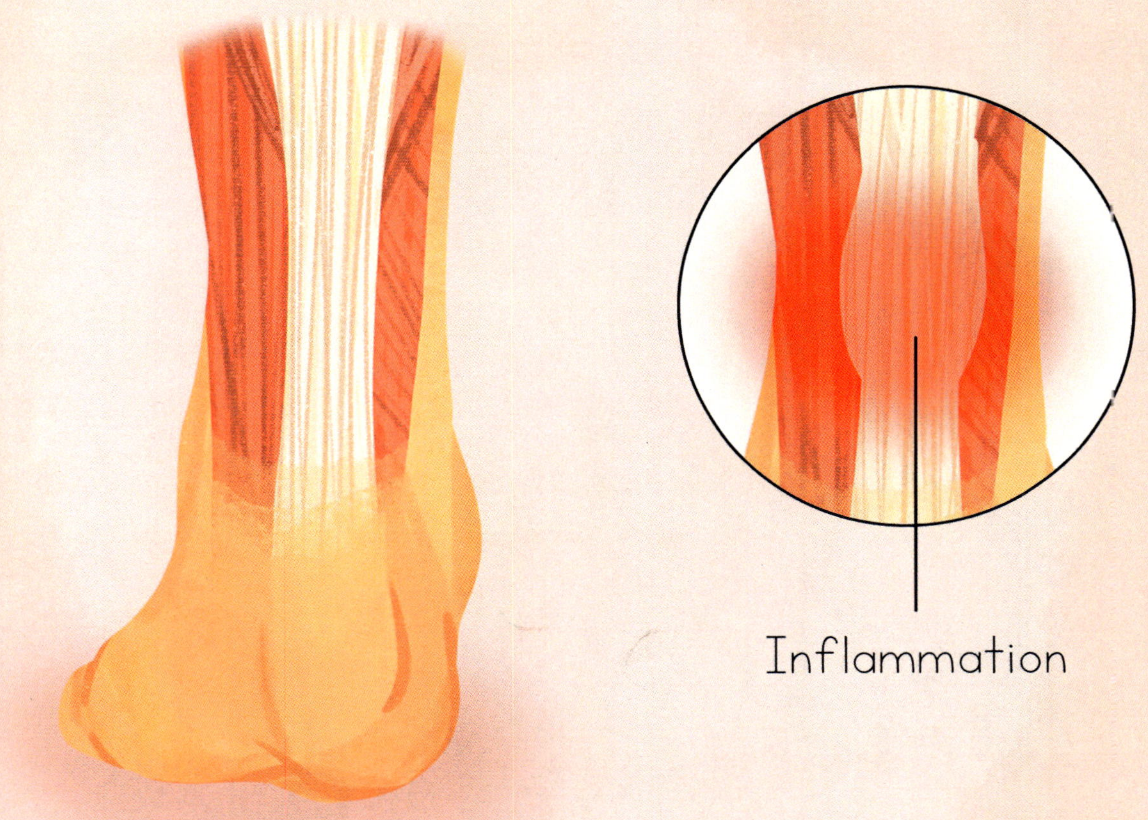

Tendonitis is inflammation or swelling of a tendon that can occur after an injury. It can be very painful!

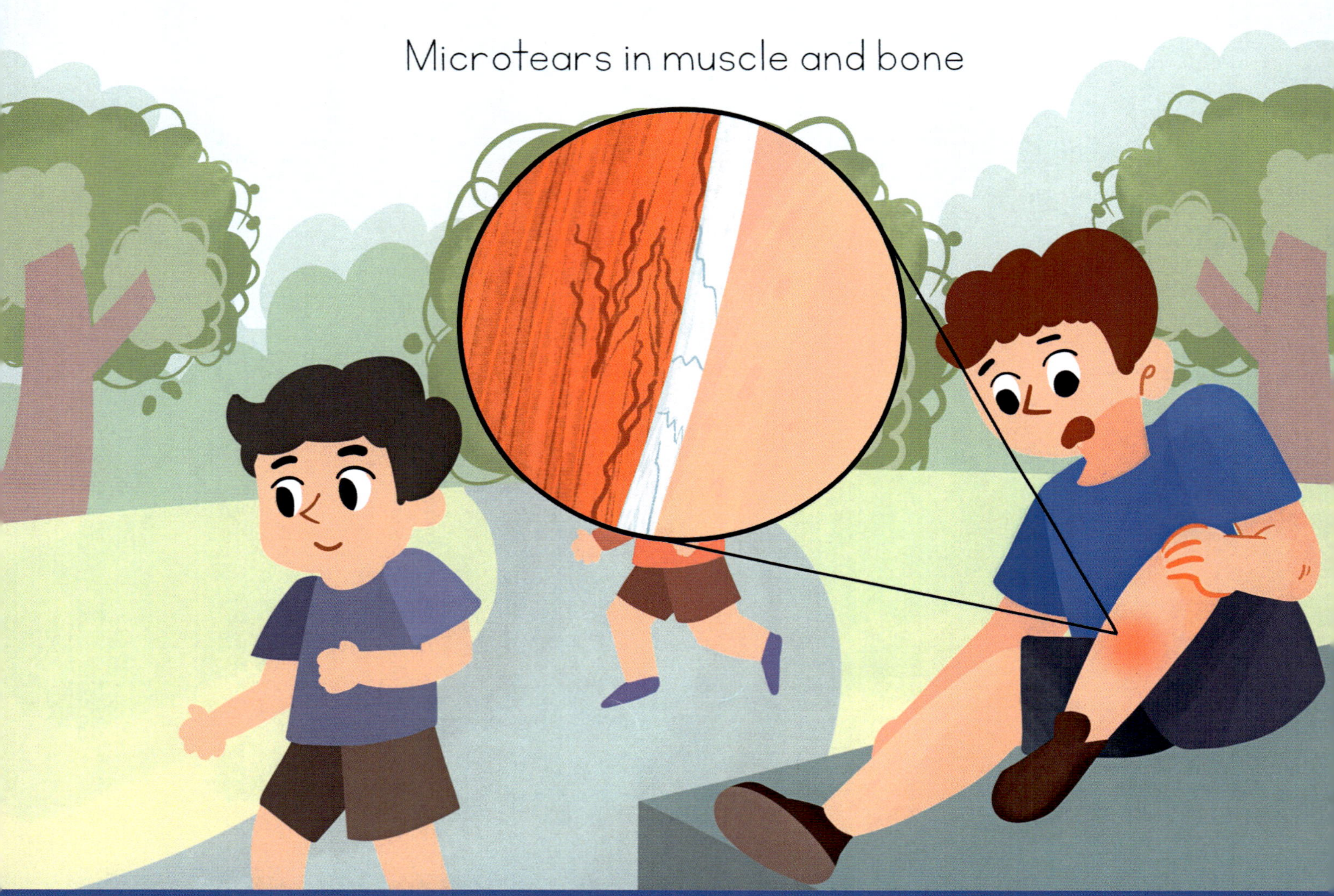

Shin splints are pain caused by overuse of the muscles, tendons, and bone tissue around our shins, usually from running.

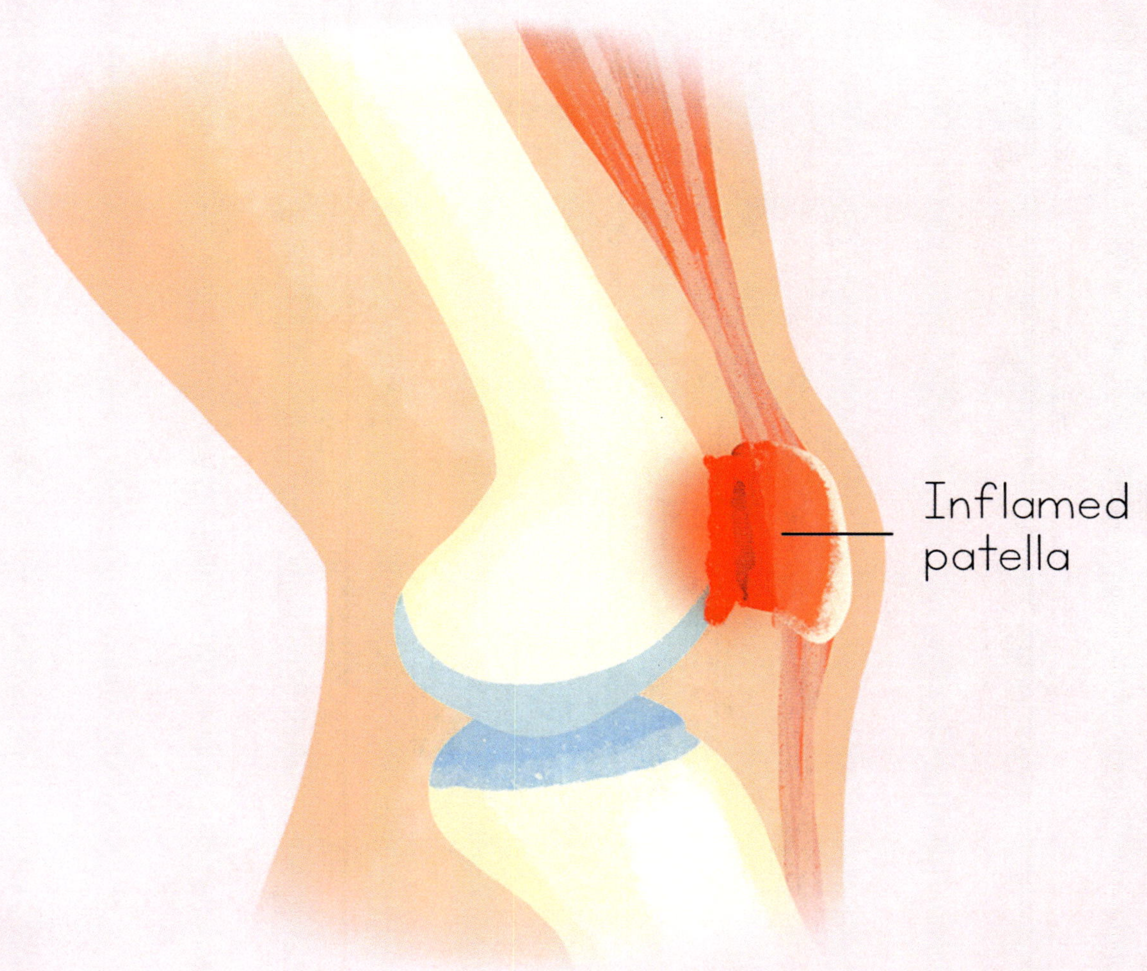

Patellofemoral pain syndrome is knee pain under or around our patella, or kneecap, caused by injury or overuse.

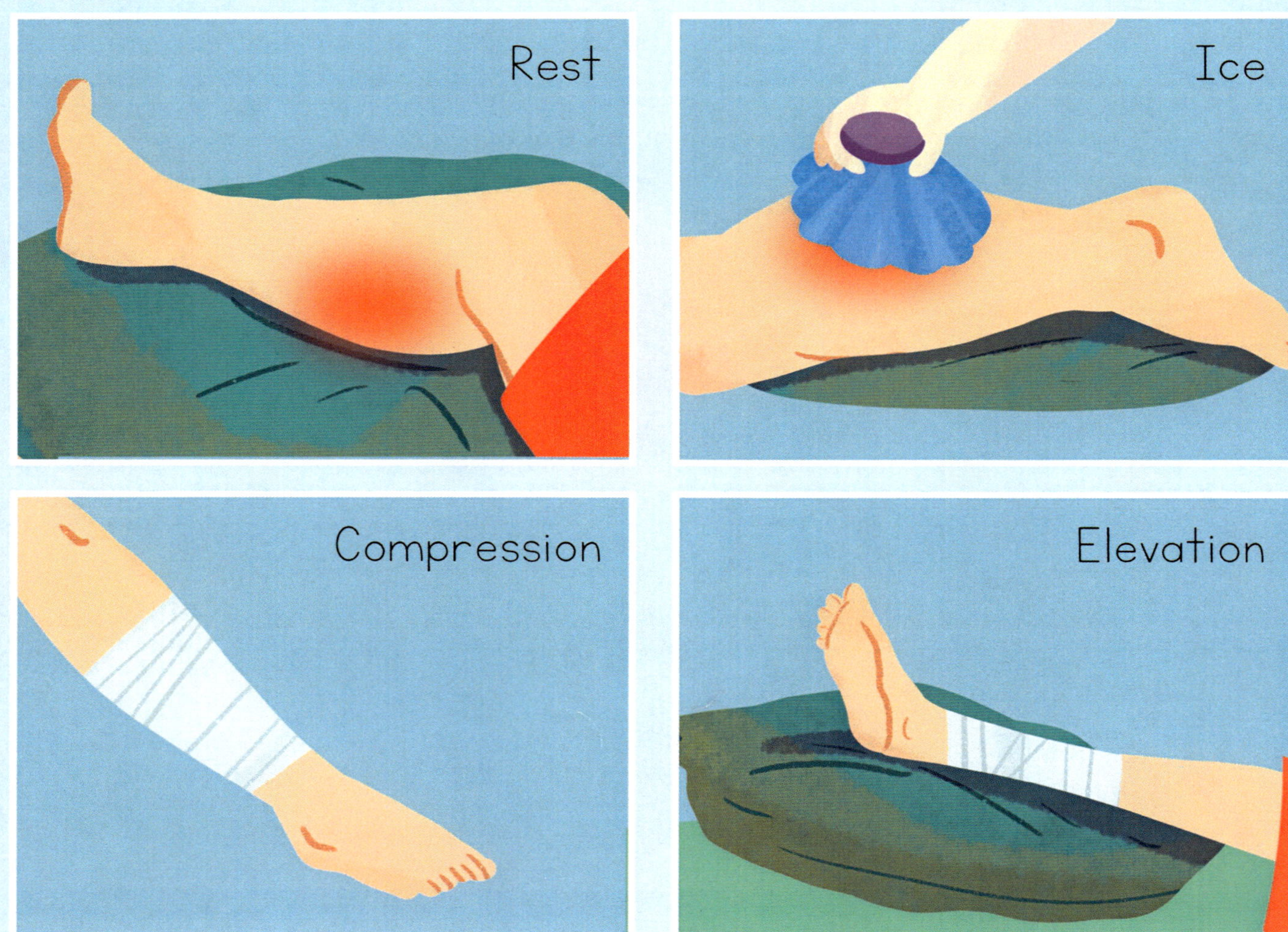

For most injuries, pain and swelling can be treated with **R**est, **I**ce, **C**ompression, and **E**levation (**RICE**).

For more severe injuries, a **physical therapist** can teach us exercises to help us get stronger and move better.

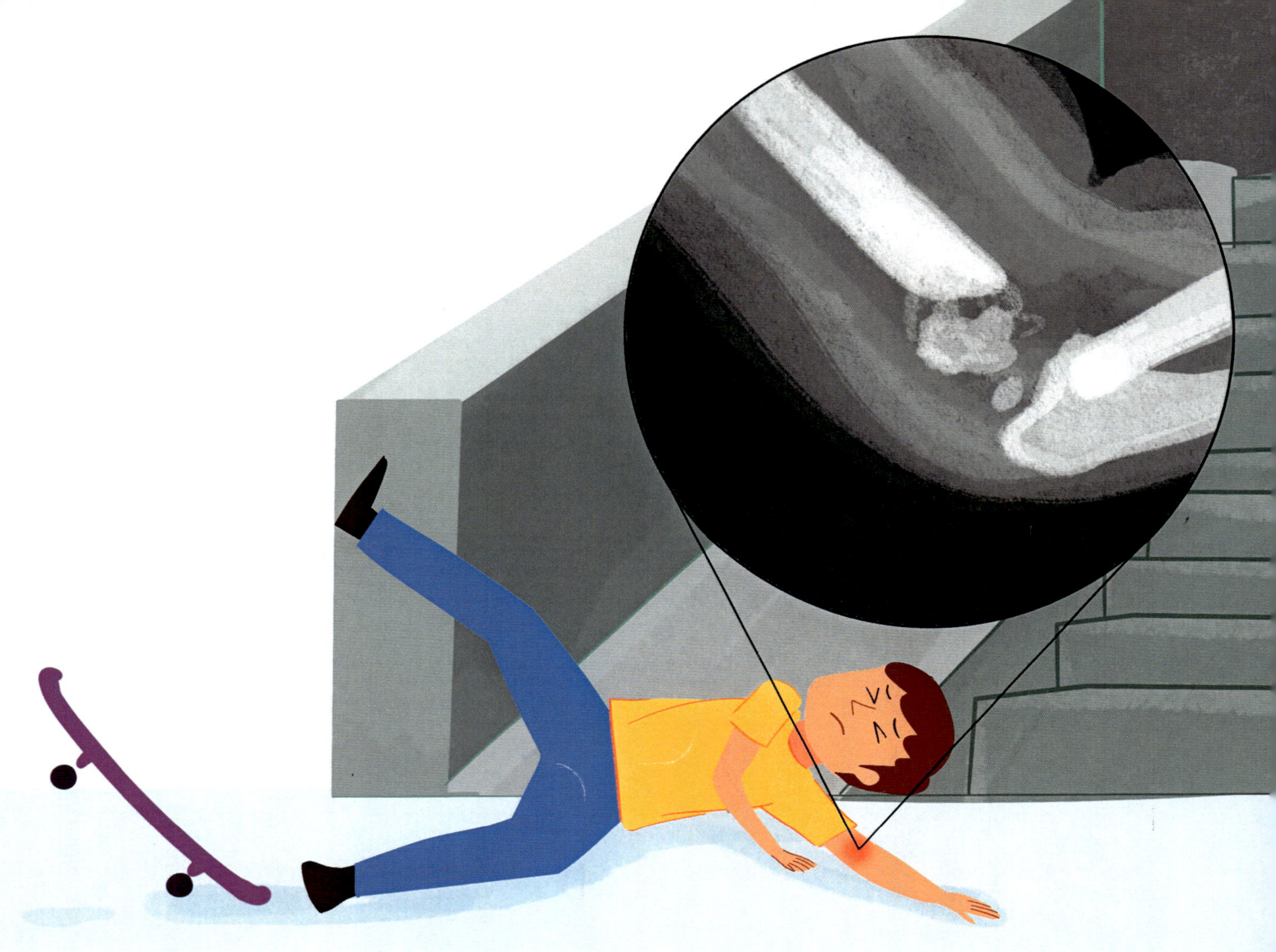

Sometimes, accidents happen and a bone can break. This is called a **fracture**.

Some fractures can be fixed by wearing a **cast**. Other fractures may need **surgery** to help them heal.

Some accidents can cause two bones
to separate where they meet at a joint.
This is called a **dislocation.**

When this happens, the bones need to be put back in their proper location by a healthcare provider. This is called a **relocation**, or reduction.

Sports medicine doctors help athletes prevent injuries by teaching them training techniques, proper nutrition, and warm-up routines.

Sports medicine doctors also determine when it's safe for athletes to resume sports after an injury. This is called **medical clearance.**

Many sports medicine doctors go to sports games to treat athletes who get injured while playing.

Adaptive sports are sports that people with and without disabilities can play, allowing everyone to have fun together!

Sports medicine doctors work on a team with nutritionists, physical therapists, orthopedic surgeons, and other healthcare professionals.

Eating a balanced diet

Getting plenty of sleep

Exercising regularly

Along with eating a balanced diet and getting plenty of sleep, exercising regularly helps keep our body healthy.

YOU'RE A FUTURE SPORTS MEDICINE DOCTOR!

Glossary

Adaptive sport (uh-DAP-tuhv): sport modified for people with disabilities

Bone (bown): hard white tissue that makes up our **skeleton**

Cartilage (KAAR-tuh-lihj): cushion that protects our joints

Dislocation (dis-low-KAY-shun): separation of two bones at a joint; can be fixed by putting the bones back into place (**relocation** or reduction)

Fracture (FRAK-shur): break in a bone; can be fixed by a **cast** or **surgery**

Joint (joynt): place where two or more bones meet

Ligament (LI-guh-muhnt): tissue that connects bone to bone

Muscle (MUH-sl): fiber that contracts to produce motion in our body; includes **skeletal muscle**, **cardiac muscle**, and **smooth muscle**

Patellofemoral pain syndrome (puh-teh-low-FEH-mr-uhl): knee pain under or around the patella, or kneecap, caused by injury or overuse

Shin splints: lower leg pain caused by overuse of muscles, tendons, and bones

Sports medicine doctor: a physician who prevents, diagnoses, and treats injuries related to physical activity; works alongside **physical therapists**, nutritionists, orthopedic surgeons, and other healthcare professionals

Sprain (sprayn): injury that occurs when a *ligament* is torn

Strain (strayn): injury that occurs when a *muscle* or *tendon* is torn

Tendon (TEN-dun): tissue that connects muscle to bone; can become inflamed or swollen (**tendonitis**)

Let's review what you learned!

1. What are physical activities or games we can play to have fun, get exercise, and compete with others? What are some examples of these?
2. What is the framework of bones that makes up our body called?
3. What are the fibers that produce motion in our body called?
4. What are the three types of muscle and their functions?
5. What is the part of our body where two or more bones meet called?
6. What protective material covers the ends of bones at joints?
7. What tissues connect bone to bone? What tissues connect bone to muscle?
8. What is a stretched or torn ligament called?
9. What is a stretched or torn muscle or tendon called?
10. What is inflammation or swelling of a tendon called?
11. How can pain and swelling in most sports-related injuries be treated? For more severe injuries, what type of health professional can teach us exercises to help us get stronger and move better?
12. What is a broken bone called? What are two ways this can be treated?
13. What are some ways sports medicine doctors help athletes prevent injuries?
14. What is the process by which a sports medicine doctor determines when it's safe for an athlete to resume playing sports called?
15. What are sports that people with and without disabilities can play called?
16. What other healthcare professionals do sports medicine doctors work with?

Your Answers

1. ______________________________
2. ______________________________
3. ______________________________
4. ______________________________
   ____
5. ______________________________
6. ______________________________
7. ______________________________
8. ______________________________
9. ______________________________
10. ______________________________
11. ______________________________
12. ______________________________
13. ______________________________
    ____
14. ______________________________
15. ______________________________
16. ______________________________

Medical School FOR KIDS™

Answer Key

1. Sports; football, basketball, baseball, and soccer
2. Skeleton
3. Muscles
4. Cardiac muscle (pumps blood to our body), smooth muscle (moves food through our gut), skeletal muscle (allows our body to move)
5. Joint
6. Cartilage
7. Ligaments; tendons
8. Sprain
9. Strain
10. Tendonitis
11. Rest, Ice, Compression, and Elevation (RICE); physical therapist
12. Fracture; cast or surgery
13. Advising athletes on proper nutrition, training techniques, and warm-up routines
14. Medical clearance
15. Adaptive sports
16. Nutritionists, physical therapists, and orthopedic surgeons

About the Authors

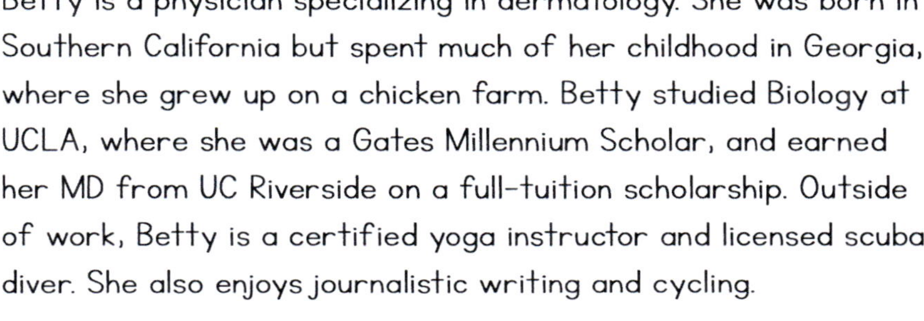

Betty is a physician specializing in dermatology. She was born in Southern California but spent much of her childhood in Georgia, where she grew up on a chicken farm. Betty studied Biology at UCLA, where she was a Gates Millennium Scholar, and earned her MD from UC Riverside on a full-tuition scholarship. Outside of work, Betty is a certified yoga instructor and licensed scuba diver. She also enjoys journalistic writing and cycling.

Dr. Betty Nguyen

Brandon is a physician specializing in ophthalmology. He was born and raised in Southern California. Brandon studied Microbiology, Immunology, and Molecular Genetics at UCLA, where he was a Barry Goldwater Scholar, and earned his MD from Stanford. He is passionate about medical education for students of all ages. In his free time, Brandon enjoys traveling, playing tennis, and performing card magic tricks.

Dr. Brandon Pham

Michelle is a physician specializing in physical medicine and rehabilitation. She was born and raised in California and studied Physiological Sciences at UCLA, where she also earned her MD. She completed physical medicine and rehabilitation residency at UC Davis in Sacramento and is currently practicing in Northern California. She likes to teach and is involved in resident medical education. Outside of work, Michelle enjoys figure skating, jogging, cycling, skiing, and spending time with her family.

Dr. Michelle Palvolgyi

Check out the rest of the books in our series!

Website: mdforkids.org

Instagram: @md.for.kids

Made in United States
North Haven, CT
20 October 2024